Best Mil

MW00999756

by Kate Carothers RN, IBCLC
illustrated by Jessica Scheberl

Katalac Books LLC

Dedications

I dedicate this book to my children for their inspiration.
    -Kate Carothers

For my Mom...to thank you for all your support, advice, and countless hours of babysitting. I absolutely could not have done this without you!
    -Jessica Scheberl

Text copyright © 2011 by Kate Carothers
Illustrations copyright © 2011 Jessica Scheberl
Edited by Lisa Carothers

Published and distributed in the United States by: Katalac Books LLC:
katalacbooks.com
Second Edition

All rights reserved. No part of this book may be reproduced by any mechanical, photographic, or electrical process, or in the form of phonographic recording; nor may it be stored in a retrieval system, transmitted, or otherwise be copied for public or private use-other than for "fair use" as brief quotations embodied in articles and reviews without prior written permission of the publisher. The intent of the author is only to offer information of a general nature to help you in your quest for successful breastfeeding. In the event you use any of the information in this book for yourself, which is your constitutional right, the author and the publisher assume no responsibility for your actions.
Library of Congress Control Number: 2010904211
ISBN 13: 978-0-615-36287-8
ISBN 10: 0-615-36287-7

www.bestmilkbook.com

Printed in the USA

Dear Parents,

My name is Kate Carothers and I am a Registered Nurse, an International Board Certified Lactation Consultant and a mother of two delightful breastfed girls. It is my passion to give families the tools they need to meet their breastfeeding goals. Best Milk will help you teach your children about breastfeeding, the healthiest and normal way to nourish your baby.

Inside Best Milk you will see examples of how to conveniently breastfeed anywhere while also including your other child/children and your partner. With the proper education and support, almost all families can reach their breastfeeding goals. Please contact a local lactation consultant or use the resources at the end of this book if you encounter any bumps in the road on your family's journey to better health.

"Come on, come on, Daddy! Hurry!"

We are getting a new baby today!

"Mommy, what are you doing with our new baby?" Mommy said, "I'm feeding her breast milk."

Best milk? I wondered.
Then Mommy explained
that best milk has everything our
baby needs to grow healthy and strong.

Mommy said that this is how baby kitties eat,

how baby elephants eat,

how baby dolphins eat,

and when I was little,

Mommy fed me best milk too!

Inside the photo album:

B A B Y

LUNCH!!

Zzzz...

feeding the ducky!!

We brought our baby
home from the hospital.

She pretty much
only eats and
sleeps right now.

Even though our baby best feeds a lot,

Mommy still has lots of time for me.

I love to play with our baby.

She really likes it
when we read to her.

Sometimes I get to help
give her a bath.

She smiles when I
count her tiny toes!

We take our baby everywhere with us.

We take her to the park.

We take her to the grocery store.

We take her to my dance class.

We even take her to the beach with us!

Our baby can't eat big people food yet.

But Mommy says best milk has all she needs.

Mommy can best feed in a chair.

She can best feed when she is lying down.

Mommy can even best
feed when she is walking!

Sometimes Mommy uses a special pumper to get the best milk out.

"Mommy, which side is going to win?"

Someday, when I'm a Mommy,
I'm going to feed my baby
best milk too.

Resources

www.kellymom.com

www.womenshealth.gov/breastfeeding

www.llli.org

www.breastfeeding.com

www.bestforbabes.org